B*WITCHED

BEHIND THE MAGIC

Nigel Cawthorne

PARRAGON

First published in 1999 by
Parragon
Queen Street House
4 Queen Street
Bath
BA1 1HE

Copyright © 1999 Parragon

Produced by Blackjacks

British Library Cataloguing-in-Publication Data

A catalogue record for this book is available from the British Library.

ISBN 0 75253 342 8

Printed in Italy

CONTENTS

Introduction

B*Witched claim their only special powers are musical. But they've cast a spell on teens all over the world. Their single 'C'est La Vie' shot to No 1 in Britain the day it was released, making them the youngest girl group to reach No 1. The twins Edele and Keavy Lynch were just 19. And their friends Lindsay Armaou and Sinead O'Caroll were 18 and 20 at the time. B*Witched's second single 'Rollercoaster' also went straight to No 1 – another record!

So did their third – 'To You I Belong'. And their fourth – 'Blame It On The Weatherman'. Their album *B*Witched* charted at No 3 and sold a million-and-a-half copies world-wide – a million in the UK. Then there's their tribute to ABBA, 'Thank ABBA For The Music', which charted in the UK at No 4 – and was a smash in Sweden.

Call them the female Hanson, or Girlzone if you want. But B*Witched are no Irish Spices. They're four denim-clad girls who play their own instruments and write their own songs. So what's the recipe for their b*witches' brew? Mix infectious melodies with a clever twist of Gaelic folk, a little bit of Blarney and the luck of the Irish.

"We're not a girl band, we're a tomboy band!" says Edele.

Keavy

Keavy-Jane Elizabeth Annie Lynch was born in Dublin on 15 December 1979. She's older than Edele, by just 20 minutes.

She was 17 when she started working in her dad's garage, and worked there for a year-and-a-half before the band got together.

"People would ask, 'Where's the tyre guy.' And I would tell them, 'You're looking at him.'" Now she owns a car of her own. It's a Golf GTI.

She always wanted to be a singer. If she had any worries she would start dancing and singing. And she can play the guitar, sax and the drums.

She says she's shy, but no one else seems to notice.

"We would sing and dance a lot at home and put on little shows all the time," she says. "There were six of us kids and we always loved to entertain."

Despite her tomboy image, Keavy is a homegirl. She wants a husband and family that's just like her mum and dad's.

"They have a great relationship," she says. "If I got married and it wasn't like that, I'd be very disappointed."

Nicknames:
Keaves
Keavers

The Lynch family are Ireland's answer to the Jacksons. There's Shane, who's in Boyzone, Tara, who is in the Irish band Fab, and 15-year-old Naomi is a dancer. And then, of course there's Keavy and Edele – the terrible twins.

The family always used to go to stay in a caravan for the summer holidays. One day, Keavy broke the window in her bedroom.

"I was terrified of what everyone would say, so I kept quiet and hoped that nobody would notice," Keavy says.

That night, there was a really bad storm, and everyone assumed that the lightning had broken it. They felt really sorry for her because they thought I must have been terrified. She never owned up.

DOUBLE

Edele has a dark secret too. At primary school, if it was raining and children arrived wet, they were allowed to go home and change. So, Edele made sure that she didn't take her umbrella when it was raining. She would stand in the rain or go into the toilets and throw water over herself - so she'd be sent home!

TROUBLE

Edele

Edele Claire Christina Edwina Lynch was born 20 minutes after her twin Keavy, on 15 December 1979. Although Keavy and Edele are identical twins, they've got very different personalities – that's why they've always gotten along so well.

"Physically, Keavy wears bangs, whereas I don't," says Edele "But when we did Top of the Pops, we wore our hair the same way and couldn't tell us apart. It was really funny."

Edele remembers her ambition to became a singer started when the family were driving around in the car when she was about nine or ten.

"I was singing 'Eternal Flame' by the Bangles and my mum and sister told me I was a great singer and that I should pursue this professionally," she says.

She also loved to dance and she studied ballet, then jazz, modern, tap dancing, then hip-hop dancing. She joined a troupe and did a lot of gigs around Ireland. Then she taught dancing for a while.

"I always knew I wanted to be a performer of some sort."

Edele loves her family, chocolate, being on stage, making the audience smile, going to bed when she is tired and eating popcorn when I'm watching a film."

She describes herself as: "level-headed, stubborn, a good friend, ambitious and a perfectionist."

But the others in B*Witched think: "She's very calm and cool."

Lindsay says: "But when she gets angry, she gets really angry! Then she just yells!"

Nicknames:
Eddie
Dele

B*Witches' Brew

Keavy and Edele were brought up in a very musical family. They were still kids when they started making up their own songs and performing them. Their dream was to become performers, but it was just a dream.

"Then, as we grew older," they say, "it started to look more realistic. We thought, 'Yeah, we can do this!'"

But for a band, they needed two more girls.

Edele and Keavy dropped out of school. Edele began working as a shop assistant and Keavy as a trainee in her father's garage. One day Sinead's car broke down outside the garage. The girls recognised each other from the Digges Lane dance studios in Dublin where they both took classes. Sinead was introduced to Edele and the group D*Zire was formed. Keavy met Lindsay at a kickboxing class. Then there were four.

They moved to Sinead's flat in Dublin and started writing songs.

"We were singing, when somebody knocked on the door," says Sinead. "We got scared because we thought we were disturbing them." But the neighbours asked them to turn up the music because it sounded so good.

The girls used to rehearse their dancing in a park, St Stephen's Green, but people often gave them strange looks.

"We had personal stereos with our music on," Sinead says. "You could see people stopping and thinking, 'Why are those girls dancing with no music'!"

Lindsay

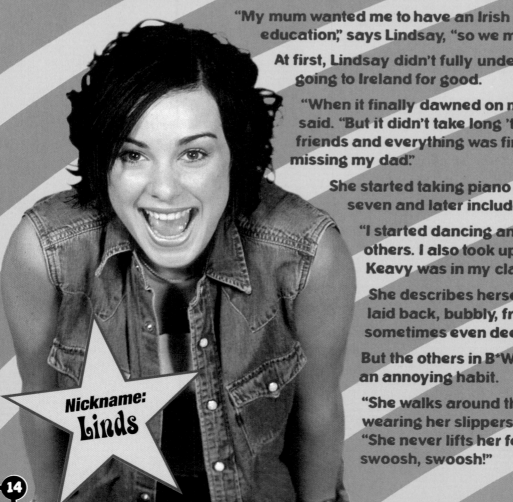

Lindsay's full name is Lindsay Gael Christian Elaine Armaou. But people seem to have a bit of a problem with the spelling. 'Lindsay' was spelt 'Linsday' on the UK edition of the 'C'est La Vie' single. And her middle name tends to be mixed up with Christina almost everywhere – even on the official B*Witched web-site!

Her mother is Irish, and her dad is Greek. Lindsay was born in Athens on 18 December 1980 where she lived until she was 13, and went to an English-speaking school there. When she was little, her favourite toy was a mini-keyboard.

"I used to play it," she says, "and when I had come up with a melody I called for my dad who had to come and listen."

But her mother wanted to move back to Ireland.

"My mum wanted me to have an Irish education," says Lindsay, "so we moved to Dublin."

At first, Lindsay didn't fully understand that they were going to Ireland for good.

"When it finally dawned on me it was awful," she said. "But it didn't take long 'til I loved it. I'd made friends and everything was fine – apart from missing my dad."

She started taking piano lessons at the age of seven and later included guitar lessons.

"I started dancing and that's how I met the others. I also took up kickboxing, and Keavy was in my class."

She describes herself as: "an ambitious, laid back, bubbly, friendly, and sometimes even deep girl".

But the others in B*Witched think she has an annoying habit.

"She walks around the house, always wearing her slippers," Sinead says. "She never lifts her feet, so they go swoosh, swoosh!"

Nickname: Linds

MAGICAL

D*Zire's break came when Irish TV were filming a documentary about the studio where the girls were rehearsing. This promoted them as the "Irish Spices" and they were soon under the wing of Boyzone's Ray Hedges. He persuaded them to change their name to B*Witched - because he found them bewitching!

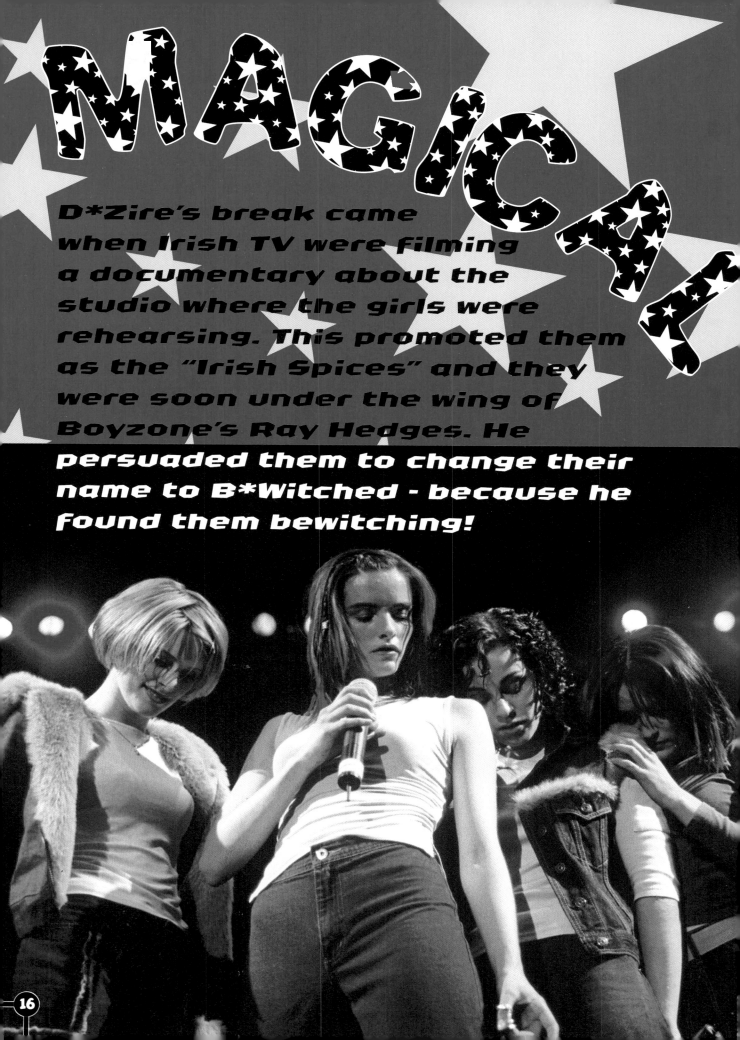

SPELLS

Manager Kim Glover first saw the girls play with Boyzone in Dublin in 1997.

"There was just a magical quality about them," she says. "They sung fantastically well, they moved well; they were just fantastic girls."

Having previously handled New Kids on the Block, Let Loose, Princess Stephanie of Monaco and PJ & Duncan, Kim knows "fantastic" when she sees it.

"Then I found out they could write songs, too," says Kim, "that was just so fantastic." She signed them to Epic.

The girls moved to London. They did a lot of radio and club appearances, plus a 'school tour' to introduce themselves for their soon-to-be-fans.

Sinead really liked it, "because we got to meet the kids who are gonna buy our music." Keavy did too. "It was great when you saw the kids dancing and singing along with us."

Then they released their debut-single 'C'est La Vie'. It went straight to No 1.

"We didn't know whether to cry or laugh!"

Sinead

Sinead Maria O'Carroll was born on 14 May 1978, in Dublin. But when she joined B*Witched she was living in Kildare, an hour outside of Dublin.

"I studied dance at the same school as Keavy, Edele and Lindsay," Sinead says.

"One day I walked into the garage where Keavy was working and we got chatting. We realised we had the same interests, so we met up and just went into the studio, and everything went from there."

She had wanted to be a performer since she was eight.

"I just knew I was going to do something in the business."

She studied drama too and was in a number of shows. With the other three girls she was soon training 30 to 34 hours a week.

"A TV station was doing a documentary on the dance centre. They asked us to appear on the show. One thing led to another and that's how we met our manager. And seven months later, they brought us to our record company. I believe in fate. I was just getting my mum's car fixed and look what happened!"

Nicknames:
Shenanigans
Socky
Skinhead

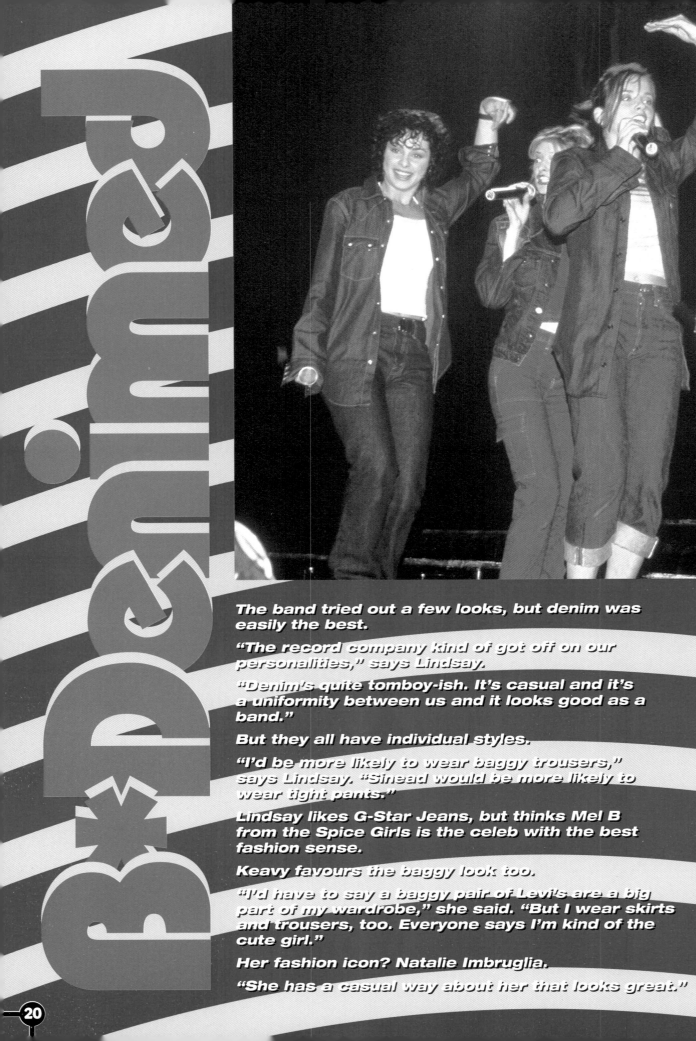

B*Denim

The band tried out a few looks, but denim was easily the best.

"The record company kind of got off on our personalities," says Lindsay.

"Denim's quite tomboy-ish. It's casual and it's a uniformity between us and it looks good as a band."

But they all have individual styles.

"I'd be more likely to wear baggy trousers," says Lindsay. **"Sinead would be more likely to wear tight pants."**

Lindsay likes G-Star Jeans, but thinks Mel B from the Spice Girls is the celeb with the best fashion sense.

Keavy favours the baggy look too.

"I'd have to say a baggy pair of Levi's are a big part of my wardrobe," she said. **"But I wear skirts and trousers, too. Everyone says I'm kind of the cute girl."**

Her fashion icon? Natalie Imbruglia.

"She has a casual way about her that looks great."

Edele could not live without her fave pair of jeans that are frayed around the edges. Her favourite designer is her mum who sometimes makes her clothes.

"We met the All Saints a couple of weeks ago and I really like their style," Edele says.

Sinead is another Natalie Imbruglia fan.

"I can't necessarily dress like that myself but she carries it off really well," says Sinead. "She makes casual clothes look really glamorous."

But Sinead admits she once wore peach corduroy dungarees with a pink jumper underneath. Peach with pink?!

Bedknobs and Broomsticks

Not to be outdone by 5ive and the Spice Girls, B*Witched have moved into a two-bedroom house in deepest Surrey.

Keavy shares a room with Lindsay. Their room has two beds, a chest of drawers, a rail instead of a wardrobe and lots of teddies.

Edele and Sinead's room is at the front of the house, so it's quite bright when the sun shines. Edele's bed is by the window and Sinead's is by the wardrobe. Edele has lots of teddies on her bed too.

"You can't see her bed for teddies," says Sinead.

"If I see a teddy machine," Edele says, "I have to win one!"

They take it in turns to cook and do the washing up. Lindsay hogs the bathroom.

"'Cos she washes her hair twice," explains Sinead.

But Sinead is always borrowing other people's stuff and claiming she put it back, while Keavy hogs the phone.

"Keavy's on the phone from 7pm to midnight," says Keavy.

"The next day people say, 'I was trying to ring you all night.'"

Her phone-bills are huuuge!

Edele, Keavy and Sinead like watching the soaps on telly, but Lindsay prefers movies.

"Nobody watches football," says Keavy, "we're so grand!"

Often they stay in and watch telly, do their nails and eat chocolate!

"Sometimes we give each other facials and Lindsay plucks everybody's eyebrows," says Sinead.

B*WITCHES' FAMILIARS

Witches are supposed to like cats, but that doesn't wash with Edele.

"Cats are boring," she says. "I hate them. I don't particularly like any animals indoors."

Which is tough because they keep chipmunks in the house.

"They're OK," says Edele, "'cos they're in a cage and you can't get to them."

"They're only small," says Keavy. "And cats and dogs run about all over the place and they wee-wee on your carpet."

But Keavy admits that kittens are cute.

"I'll tell you why I'm not keen on animals in the house," says Edele. "When I was a kid, my friend's huge red setter knocked me over and pinned me down. Urgh."

Lindsay is the real animal lover. She has two cats called Leah and Snoopy, and three dogs called Husky, Cheeky and Chubby.

The others more than compensate with their teddies. Edele has millions.

"My favourite teddy's called Patch," Edele says.

"I have loads too," says Keavy. "There's bunny the hot water bottle, Alfie who Edele bought for me and my teddy bear slippers."

"Well, I have a white polar bear who's so cuddly," says Sinead.

But Keavy says it's horrible.

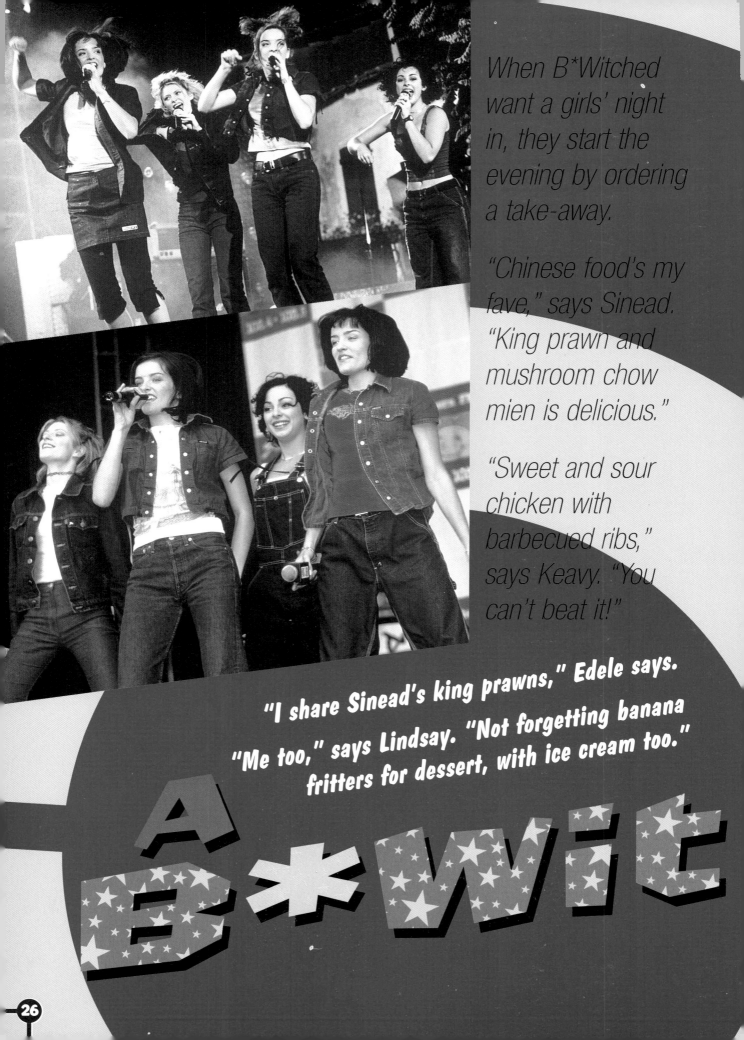

When B*Witched want a girls' night in, they start the evening by ordering a take-away.

"Chinese food's my fave," says Sinead. "King prawn and mushroom chow mien is delicious."

"Sweet and sour chicken with barbecued ribs," says Keavy. "You can't beat it!"

"I share Sinead's king prawns," Edele says. "Me too," says Lindsay. "Not forgetting banana fritters for dessert, with ice cream too."

A B*Wit

While they're waiting for the food, they entertain themselves with a few phone pranks.

"Nothing cruel – we just ring our mates or boys we fancy and pretend to be someone else. It's a real Bart Simpson thing to do!"

When the food comes, they forget all that lah-di-dah business about sitting around a dinner table. Instead, they get comfy with cushions and eat in front of the TV. Then they pamper themselves.

"Boys really miss out on the fun, not wearing make-up."

Sinead puts Aretha Franklin on the stereo. Keavy likes anything charty and bouncy, like All Saints or 5ive. Edele likes Ultra, while Lindsay favours the Jackson Five.

"Definitely no soppy tunes, 'cause they'd make us cry and mess up our makeovers!"

Sinead likes to lounge in blue thermals. Keavy wears pink silk pyjamas.

Edele slobs out in a big shirt, while Lindsay dons trackie bottoms and an old T-shirt.

"We have a video marathon. First a romance, then a comedy, then a scary film just before we go to sleep."

If they get too relaxed they have an energetic game of Twister.

Sometimes they get peckish again and call up for a take-away mushroom and pineapple pizza with garlic bread. Then snuggle up to watch the rest of the vids and veg out.

Chilling Night In

The first boy Keavy kissed was called Ducks. He was Shane's friend from Portugal. Keavy was about 12 and remembers being very nervous. Then when she was 16, she kissed her friend Peggy-Ann's cousin.

The first boy Edele kissed was one of her brother's friends – just like Keavy. It wasn't the same guy though. She was 13. Later she was working in a sports shop.

"We had our Christmas party and I snogged this boy I worked with," she says. "But I think every girl at the place kissed that boy that night."

Both the twins broke up with their boyfriends when they moved to London.

B✳Loved

Sinead had her first kiss when was 15. She was sitting on the school bus with the guy.

Lindsay's first snog was in Hong Kong.

"I was visiting a friend there and there was this guy she'd been telling me about for months. She said: 'You two are made for each other. You really ought to get together.' She'd been going on about him for so long that I kinda stopped listening... until I saw him. He was so gorgeous I couldn't take my eyes off him and I ended up kissing him."

So who do they most fancy?

Keavy: "Mel Gibson. But he's married – a younger, single Mel Gibson!"

Sinead: "Luke Perry and George Clooney."

Lindsay: "Jim Carrey. He makes me laugh."

Edele: "Brad Pitt – but he's taken!"

Only Lindsay likes bad boy Robbie Williams.

"A bad boy doesn't turn me on," says Edele. "I can't be bothered with boys with an attitude."

Casting Spells

If Keavy could cast a magical spell on the world, there would be no war, no fighting, no homeless people and everyone would be happy. Failing that she would cast a spell to make Brad Pitt fall in love with her.

Sinead's spell would be to stop poverty and give everyone food and water.

She would also stop winter!

Lindsay claims she already has magical powers. Like a proper witch she has the ability to communicate with cats.

"I seem to understand them," she says. "I've always had cats and I used to sit and talk to them and I know what all their different movements mean. I think I was a cat in a previous life."

If she owned a witch's broom, Lindsay would fly to Greece to see her dad. Edele would love to fly to the moon. Sinead would fly to the Caribbean. "'Cos I've only ever seen it on TV," she says. "I've never really seen white sand and completely clear blue sea before."

Keavy would like to fly under the sea.

"People are always trying to find out about space but there's another world down there." She would also like to turn her old boyfriend into a frog – or rather, a tadpole.

Edele says she would prefer to turn herself into a frog to see what it was like.

Into the Crystal Ball

The history of pop is littered with once-successful acts who broke up at the height of their fame. And girl groups are notoriously fragile things.

The Spice Girls have put up with management problems, the loss of a key member and motherhood, while All Saints sacked their manager amid rumours of internal disharmony.

But B*Witched have been taking advice from older and wiser heads, including the Bee Gees and Celine Dion.

"Celine came over and said in her French accent, 'Oh, C'est la Vie!'," says Lindsay. "And then she said to us, 'You must stick together. Don't let anything split you up.'"

But as yet, there are no such clouds on the shiny, happy, B*Witched horizon.